STOP ABUSING OUR LANGUAGE

SPEAK BETTER ENGLISH - COMMON MISTAKES
REVEALED AND CORRECTED

CLIVE SEIGAL

ABOUT THE AUTHOR

The author was born in England and went to Radley College before reading English at Rhodes University, South Africa. Living in England in recent years , he has perceived a steady deterioration in the quality of our spoken language as heard throughout the media today. He has written this short book in a desperate effort to arrest this decline.

© Copyright 2020 - Clive Seigal - All rights reserved.

The content contained within this book may not be reproduced, duplicated or transmitted without direct written permission from the author or the publisher.

The content contained within this book may not be reproduced, duplicated or transmitted without direct written permission from the author or the publisher.

Under no circumstances will any blame or legal responsibility be held against the publisher, or author, for any damages, reparation, or monetary loss due to the information contained within this book, either directly or indirectly. You are responsible for your own choices, actions, and results.

Legal Notice:

This book is copyright protected. This book is only for personal use. You cannot amend, distribute, sell, use, quote or paraphrase any part, or the content within this book, without the consent of the author or publisher.

Disclaimer Notice:

Please note the information contained within this document is for educational and entertainment purposes only. Every effort has been made to present accurate, enduring and reliable information. No warranties of any kind are declared or implied. Readers acknowledge that the author is not engaging in the rendering of legal, financial, medical or professional advice. The content within this book has been derived from various sources. Please consult a licensed professional before attempting any techniques outlined in this book.

By reading this document, the reader agrees that under no circumstances is the author responsible for any losses, direct or indirect, which are incurred as a result of the use of the information contained within this document, including, but not limited to, errors, omissions, or inaccuracies.e or legal responsibility be held against the publisher, or author, for any damages, or monetary loss due to the information contained within this book. Either directly or indirectly. You are responsible for your own choices, actions, and results.

ANNOUNCEMENT

Before you read any further, **PLEASE NOTE**:-

This book is all about the **spoken** word. It explains typical grammatical errors and deals with them. It is impossible to convey via the **written** word all the nuances encompassing correct speech.

Therefore, I shall soon be making an audible version of this book.

Meanwhile, I can send you an audio snippet. This explains my reasons for writing *Stop Abusing Our Language* and contains a few general hints about speaking plus a selection of commonly mispronounced, everyday words.

I suggest you apply ASAP for this essential audio snippet by going to:
https://cliveseigal.activehosted.com/f/15

AUTHOR'S NOTE

Because *Stop Abusing Our Language* is more of an explanatory manual than a normal book, there are many embellishments to the script. These are required so as to draw the reader's attention in varying degrees of urgency to the significance of the particular points being made.

Quotation marks are used regularly because there are so many instances of dialogue. The examples have been concocted for illustrative purposes. Many are pretty ghastly but most of them occur only too often in real life. Quotation marks may also be used to denote words or even letters of specific importance. Occasionally, where quotation marks are not appropriate, words may be underlined for emphasis. They may even be capitalised for additional clout.

Specific words chosen for discussion are normally emboldened for extra clarity. Italics are used when naming books or, in one case, a boat.

CONTENTS

Introduction … xi

1. Sit/Stand; Lie/Lay … 1
2. As Though – not Like; Is/Are – Was/Were (Matching Singular/Plural) … 4
3. Unique; Rubbish; Good/Well; I/Me (Pronoun Cases) … 7
4. Of; "Down the Pub"; Comparisons … 11
5. With/Than/To etc. - Using the Right Prepositions … 15
6. Similar Words but Different Meanings - Don't Be Confused … 18
7. American Anomalies … 24
8. Society and "Class" Issues … 26
9. Evolved Meanings … 34
10. Pronunciation and Articulation … 38

Conclusion … 43
Bibliography … 45
Appendix … 47

INTRODUCTION

It was while I was on a peaceful walk along the spectacular Dorset cliffs that I was abruptly brought to my senses as I emerged from a small wood. A scruffy lad jumped up in front of me exclaiming bitterly "Ouch – I think I was sat on an 'ornet's nest!" Any sympathy I should have had for the victim was nullified by his horrible grammar. As I hear more and more of this sort of language all over the media, lingering pity for the ignorant perpetrators has turned to anger and loss of respect. Surely we all want to convey our thoughts with confidence and self-esteem.

Sad to say, there has been a marked deterioration in the quality of the English language as it is spoken today. Of course, written English is also riddled with errors but that is another story. It is the spoken word which I am going to address in this book. That

INTRODUCTION

will be English as spoken according to grammar developed in the United Kingdom and promulgated throughout the British Commonwealth. I shall be pointing out selected examples of the most common and annoying indiscretions which I fear have become widespread these days. At the very least, **we must be aware of these errors**. It is extremely disturbing that our wonderful language is being abused – even, dare I say it, by the B.B.C. which no longer seems to require acceptable basic standards of grammar and pronunciation from its broadcasters.

I have been listening to people speaking English for over 70 years, whether it be on the wireless (now more commonly known as the radio), on television, or simply in everyday conversation. During this time, the spoken word has suffered in two contrasting ways. First, and this is rather sad, most of the old regional dialects have been watered down to such an extent that they are no longer discernible (at least this has been tempered by the increased number of foreign accents often heard now just about everywhere). And second - but much more alarming than dwindling dialects - is the increasing prevalence of faulty grammar. This is no longer confined to the illiterates of our society but now seems to be spreading to the so-called educated classes. The purpose of this discourse is to bring to your attention some of the more glaring examples – and try to remedy them.

Examples are not discussed in any obvious logical order -

though they may well be treated in decreasing order of exasperation caused. Whatever, for ease of reference, each chapter's heading indicates most of the contentious issues contained therein.

1

SIT/STAND; LIE/LAY

Let's start with "**Sit**". I find the misuse of this verb especially infuriating. English verbs normally have two forms to determine the present tense. These signify the finite present and the ongoing or continuing present – in this case – **sit** and **sitting**. e.g.

1. "We **sit** down because we are tired."
2. "We are **sitting** down because we are tired" – NOT "We are **sat** down"…

The problem arises even more often when the ongoing present is put into the past – i.e.

3. "We **sat** down because we were tired" (finite past).

4. "We were **sitting** down because we were tired" – NOT "We were **sat** down"... (so often heard!).

"We were **sat** down" actually means we were **sat** down by someone else. e.g.

"We were **sat** down on the bench by the irate policeman." It is still a clumsy sentence as is so often the case when the passive is used. Were this the actual meaning intended, it would be better to say "the irate policeman **sat** us down on the bench".

The verb "stand" is often similarly abused, though here it is confined to incorrect usage in the past tense when **"stood"** becomes the critical word. e.g.

"He **stood** in the doorway to block her escape" - (totally correct).

"He **was standing** in the doorway to block her escape" - (equally acceptable).

"He **was stood** in the doorway to block her escape" - (horrible!). Unless the literal meaning is intended (unlikely!): i.e. he was placed in the doorway by someone else to block her escape.

The verbs "Lie" and "Lay" can have much the same meaning but are sometimes used incorrectly. The essential difference is that "lie" is intransitive and therefore does not require an object. Whereas "lay" is a transitive verb and so must have an object.

The confusion arises because the past tense of "lie" is "lay" and it is vital to be aware of this when using the ongoing form of both words – i.e. "ing". e.g. (using "**lie**")

(a) "He **lies** down because he is tired" (present).

(b) "He **lay** down because he was tired" (past).

(c) "He was **lying** down because he was tired" - NOT "He was laying down"... (also often heard!)

Equally wrong would be "He is laying down" or "He is going to lay down". There is no object and so "lie" must be used. This is extremely important to grasp.

e.g. (using "**lay**")

(a) "He **lays** the table for dinner" (present).
(b) "He **laid** the table for dinner" (past).
(c) "He was **laying** the table for dinner."

The correct use of "**lay**" is pretty obvious. Just remember it must always have an object.

2

AS THOUGH – NOT LIKE; IS/ARE – WAS/WERE (MATCHING SINGULAR/PLURAL)

Let's consider another point of grammar which seems to have become almost universally accepted in spite of clearly being incorrect. This is the lazy use of "**like**" instead of "**as though**". Predominantly used after the verbs "look" or "seem", "**like**" is wrong – "**as though**" is right (or "**as if**" is also acceptable). e.g.

"It looks **as though** he's not coming" – NOT "It looks **like** he's not coming".

The rule is that "like" should be followed by a noun but must not be used to introduce a verbal clause. e.g.

"He plays **like** an expert" – or

"He plays **as though** he's an expert" – but NOT "He plays **like** he's an expert".

Sadly, more and more supposedly educated people no longer make this distinction.

Now for some more blunders: take the most basic English verb of all – to "**be**".

In the present tense, "**is**" denotes the singular, "**are**" the plural. e.g.

"There **is** one person on that bus." Any more than one and "**are**" should be used. e.g.

"There **are** four people on that bus." BUT "There **is** four"... is often heard.

And this mistake seems to be especially common when the shortened form is used. i.e.

"**There's** four of us on this bus" – instead of "t**here're** four of us on this bus".

In the past tense, "**was**" denotes the singular, "**were**" the plural. e.g.

"We **were** in a great hurry to see the whale breaching" - (correct). NOT "We **was** in a great hurry"... (awful).

This may all seem trivial but, to me, glaring errors such as these are destroying our spoken language. I mean, if we can't be bothered to match singular with singular and plural with plural, then I despair. Most such slapdash mistakes should be easy to rectify with a bit of care and thought.

However, there are more complicated examples which can trap many of the less wary. Collective nouns fall into this category. These are singular nouns which refer to a group of people, animals or things. e.g. (people):

"The crowd **was** enormous" (NOT **were**). This is pretty obvious. Likewise, "the crowd of demonstrators **was** enormous" (again NOT **were**). Less obvious this time because, without due care, the subject may be misconstrued. And it is the subject which determines the case of the verb – i.e. singular or plural. "Crowd" (singular) remains the subject – not "demonstrators" (plural).

e.g. (animals): "This herd of cattle **was** not producing enough milk" (NOT **were**).

e.g. (things): "The collection of antiques **was** not very valuable" (NOT **were**).

The pronoun "none" can be confusing. e.g.

"**Not one** sweet **was** left in the bag" is obviously correct. But "**none was** left in the bag" is also correct (NOT "**none were** left in the bag") - far less obvious. "**Was**" is right because "**none**" is effectively short for "**not one**". i.e. "**Not one** sweet **was** left in the bag" is clearly correct. Whereas "**not one** sweet were left in the bag" is clearly wrong.

3

UNIQUE; RUBBISH; GOOD/WELL; I/ME (PRONOUN CASES)

Now for a few words or expressions which are often used incorrectly.

Unique is an adjective which means "only one of its kind". A thing or object is either unique or not unique. It is an absolute state and so cannot be qualified. i.e.

Something cannot be "quite unique" or "nearly unique" or "completely unique".

It is worth mentioning here that unique is the most prominent of a number of adjectives sometimes known as "absolutes". Such words describe an absolute state which therefore cannot be quantified. Nor can they take the comparative or superlative form (cf. "Comparisons" in ch. 4). Other examples, not all as convincing as **unique,** are first and last, wet and dry, dead and alive. These are all technically "absolutes" but I think one can get away with expressions such as "nearly dead" or "almost dry" without disturbing any but the most ardent pedants.

Rubbish is a noun – NOT an adjective. After a humiliating defeat, a supporter may declare "we were rubbish" or, worse still, "we **was** rubbish". Of course, we fully understand the feeling of frustration expressed by the supporter – but it's terrible English! However, the use of "rubbish" as an adjective has become so widespread in colloquial English that it seems to have become legitimised, even in many reputable dictionaries. e.g.

"He was a rubbish schoolmaster" or "It was a rubbish play" - apparently acceptable nowadays but, to my mind, deplorable.

Good or **Well** – the simple answer to the commonest question of all: "How are you?". There used to be no doubt as to how this welcoming question should be answered (unless you were obviously quite ill) - "Very well, thank you" or perhaps less formally - "fine, thanks". But a strange reply (or it seems strange to me) has become increasingly popular - "good, thanks" or "I'm good". It would appear that such an answer has the same meaning as "well" so why not use the correct word? It is true that "good" can have a variety of meanings but, in this context, its logical meaning would be to express the opposite of "bad" or "naughty". I'm probably being too critical as usual and should just accept that "good" here is the modern short form for "I'm in a good state of health", clearly an absurd way to answer the original question "How are you?".

I or **Me** – subject or object. More and more often I hear people starting a sentence "Me and my mother/friend/dog...". This is both incorrect and impolite and must be avoided. It could be said that some of the mistakes mentioned above are merely insignificant quibbles which often seem to have become perfectly acceptable in modern society. But starting a sentence with the object form is a genuine howler. e.g.

"**Me** and my mother took **him** for a walk" is wrong on two counts. First, "Me and my mother" form the combined subject and "Him for a walk" is the object (or, more correctly, the objectival phrase). The subject pronoun here is, of course, "**I**" so this should replace "**Me**" in the example sentence. Second, it is also polite (and usually right) to put oneself after others in most instances – and certainly in this case. So the correct version is "My mother and **I** took **him** for a walk". The sentence can be reversed, of course, in which case the wording becomes "**He** took my mother and **me** for a walk". The same logic applies for all pronouns.

Not many English words have different cases to determine whether they are the subject or object of a verb but pronouns are the exception, especially in the first and third persons.

I or me (1st singular, subject or object); we or us (1st plural, subject or object).

You (2nd person singular and plural, unchanging).

He, she, it or him, her, it (3rd singular, subject or object); they or them (3rd plural, subject or object).

The correct choice of pronoun should come naturally to native English speakers. However, there is one prominent pronoun, "who" (subject) or "whom" (object), which seems almost to have lost its object case. It appears that even quite intelligent people consider the use of "whom" to be archaic. Please be aware that it remains correct practice to use "whom" when the accusative form is required by a preposition or verb. e.g.

"The girl to **whom** he had given an unexpected lift was extremely grateful."

"The girl **whom** he had just chastised would not stop crying."

To use "who" in either of the above examples would undeniably be wrong.

4

OF; "DOWN THE PUB"; COMPARISONS

Of – necessary or redundant? The problem is that there are no obvious rules to resolve this question. It must be particularly difficult for those learning English as a second language. For native speakers it should become instinctive.

There are circumstances where the use of "**of**" is necessary and others where it is not. A case in point (of the second variety), disturbingly common in recent times, is the unnecessary use of "of" after "outside" (or "inside"). e.g.

"He was hiding outside the back door" is concise and correct. "He was hiding outside **of** the back door" is wrong. "**Of**" just isn't required and yet it is so often added in this context and I don't understand why.

Conversely, there are occasions where "**of**" is essential and yet is often omitted. One such case which immediately comes to mind is in conjunction with the verb "throw". e.g.

"He threw it out the window" is horrible. "**Of**" must be used here: "He threw it out **of** the window" is right. What about "He got out the car"? What does this actually mean? "**Got**" is seldom a good word to use and is to be avoided wherever possible. "He got out the car" should mean something like "He brought/drove out the car" (from the garage, perhaps). It should not mean "He got out **of** the car" but I'm afraid that is by far the more likely intended interpretation. The use of the verb "get/got" is frowned upon in many circumstances but is difficult to avoid when describing the act of entering or leaving a car. "He disembarked (or alighted) from the car" sounds stupid; whereas it would be acceptable if describing the leaving of a ship (or aeroplane).

Continuing with the "**of**" theme, there is the difficulty with "composed" and "comprised" which both mean, essentially, "made up of". This is another example of the "**of**" conundrum. "Composed" requires "**of**" - "comprised" does not. e.g.

"The group was composed **of** five boys and two girls" (correct).

"The group comprised five boys and two girls" (equally correct).

"The group was comprised **of** five boys and two girls" (wrong!).

Another popular expression comes to mind: "He's down the pub" or "He's gone down the pub" - statements with a hint of humour which may help hide the lazy English being used. He is either "**at** the pub" or "he's gone down **to** the pub" (or he's just "gone **to** the pub" - unless the pub is actually at a lower altitude!). In this context, "down" seems to have lost its literal meaning – i.e. the opposite of "up".

I'm probably being too pedantic. It depends how seriously we want to take the maintenance of acceptable spoken English. I believe accurate speech is normally desirable unless we are striving for humour or ambiguity.

Comparisons can cause problems if an essential fact is not grasped (I'll explain this after giving you a quick introduction). Most adjectives can be expressed in three ways to determine degrees of comparison. e.g. (Take "big")

1. "John's car is big" (basic description).
2. "John's car is bigg**er** than David's" (this is the comparative - **er** is the suffix).
3. "John has the bigg**est** car in the group" (this is the superlative situation - **est** is the suffix).

What then is the "essential fact" already mentioned? It is to be found in the third example - "John has the bigg**est** car in the group" - which signifies that there must be at least **three** cars in contention. If only two are being compared, then the comparative form must be used - "John's car is the bigg**er**" - Not "the bigg**est**". The important rule, often abused, is that use of the superlative form of an adjective is necessary only when at least **three** objects are being compared. e.g. (Take "beautiful" - where use of the **er** and **est** suffixes would be clumsy)

1. "Anne was beautiful."
2. "Mary was **more** beautiful than Anne."
3. "Jane was the **most** beautiful girl on parade" (at least three girls must have been in contention).

Again, simple examples of comparison but this time using **more** and **most**.

BUT please take note (cf. 2. above) - **two** girls are being discussed here, Anne and Mary. "Anne is pretty but Mary is the putti**er**" - NOT "...the puttest".

Out of interest, you may also like to note two very common adjectives whose comparative forms change completely - "good, better, best" and "bad, worse, worst".

5

WITH/THAN/TO ETC. - USING THE RIGHT PREPOSITIONS

C**ompare**. Certain words need to be followed by particular prepositions. Sometimes alternative words can be perfectly acceptable but will suggest a subtle difference in meaning. Take "compare" - which can be followed by **"to"** or **"with"** depending on the precise meaning intended. Comparing **"to"** suggests a likening of one thing to something else. e.g.

"The carnage caused by the hurricane was compared **to** the scene of a major air crash."

When simply comparing like with like or establishing a comparison, then "with" should be used. e.g.

"Nowadays, some of England's best sparkling wines can confidently be compared **with** Champagne."

Bored. "We were all bored **with** the sermon." "**With**" after bored please – NOT "**of**". One is normally bored "**with**" something, never "**of**" it but occasionally "**by**" it. "**By**" can follow "bored" if there is a particular reason for the boredom. "We were all bored by the vicar's persistent stammer during the sermon."

Similar/Different. "Apart from being torn, her dress was **similar to** her sister's." "**To**" follows "**similar**" in all situations but its antonym "**different**" can be far more problematical.

Although "**different**" can be followed by "**from**", "**to**" or "**than**", I consider "**from**" to be correct. "**To**" is now frowned upon, whereas "**than**" is distinctly American and not acceptable outside the States.

"**Fed up**" is another expression that must be followed by "**with**" and not "**than**" or "**of**" which would both be Americanisms.

There are other instances where "**than**" is incorrectly used instead of "as". e.g.

"More tourists **than** ever came to London last year." Nothing wrong there – but:

"Twice as many tourists came to London **than** last year" is ugly.

"T**han**" can be left out (or replaced by "**as**"): "Twice as many tourists came to London last year."

Although there is nothing wrong with the grammar here, the meaning lacks clarity. Is it twice as many as the previous year or twice as many as the current year? To make this distinction, something has to be added. This can be "Twice as many tourists came to London last year **as** the previous year" or "... **as** this year". But NOT "**than** the previous year" or "**than** this year". Why not? Because if "**as**" has been used already in the sentence then it must be used again. "**Than**" must be replaced with "**as**" or omitted. If a word can be left out without affecting the meaning, then it is usually preferable to leave it out. The old motto "keep it short and simple" is seldom wrong for both the spoken and written form.

6

SIMILAR WORDS BUT DIFFERENT MEANINGS - DON'T BE CONFUSED

I have noticed several pairs of words which often seem to be confused. This is obviously not an exhaustive list but I have tried to pick out examples which tend to occur disturbingly often.

Affect or **Effect** – **affect** can only be a verb; **effect** can be a verb and a noun. **Affect** has two different meanings; it can mean "putting on an act". e.g.

"He **affected** an exaggerated French accent in the style of Inspector Clouseau."

But "**affect**" is more often used to produce a result or have an **effect** on someone or something (the source of the confusion, perhaps). e.g.

"The alcohol had clearly **affected** his judgement."

The noun "**effect**" is used to bring about a subsequent action or result. e.g

"The **effect** of his drunken driving was the loss of his licence."

In the plural, "**effects**" means "personal possessions".

The verb "**effect**" means "to get something done". e.g.

"He **effected** the deal with a crucial telephone call."

Complement or Compliment – both can be nouns or verbs but their meanings differ. "**Complement**" relates to complete. e.g.

"The club had a full **complement** of coaching staff."

A "**compliment**" is an expression of praise for a person. e.g.

"He **complimented** her on her athletic prowess."

Apart from its connection with human merit, used as an adjective, **complimentary** has taken on an additional meaning – free of charge. e.g.

"Members were entitled to a **complimentary** cup of coffee." They didn't have to pay for it.

However, "most members enjoy a **complementary** glass of wine with their meal" simply states that fact. (After all, wine and food do tend to **complement** each other.) It does not imply that the wine would be free. (Mind you, they'd enjoy it all the more if it were.)

Disinterested or **Uninterested** – these have different meanings and should not be muddled.

Disinterested means unbiased – not favouring one side more than another. However, being **disinterested** does not necessarily show lack of interest. Indeed, umpires and referees should be **disinterested** even though they are required to show maximum interest in the game which they are controlling.

Uninterested means "having no interest" and must be used exclusively when this meaning is required. The two words are NOT interchangeable.

Flaunt or **Flout** – both useful verbs with completely different meanings. To **flaunt** is to make a display of something in an arrogant manner. e.g.

"He **flaunted** his new car by driving slowly past his neighbour and sounding the horn."

To **flout** is to disregard a law, rule or convention with contempt. e.g.

"He deliberately **flouted** the 'No Entry' sign even though he knew a policeman was watching."

Gourmand or **Gourmet** – both are French words relating to food which have become commonly used in English (particularly "gourmet") because our language has no adequate equivalents. A "**gourmand**" is likely to be obsessed with food and probably very greedy. A "**gourmet**" is an expert in the appreciation of fine food and wine. e.g.

"The **gourmand** wolfed down the complete steak while the **gourmet** was still enthusing about his first mouthful."

Imply or **Infer** – similar words whose meanings can easily be confused. **Imply** means to suggest or create an impression that something is apparent or likely to happen (without actual proof). **Infer** is to deduce a situation as a result of specific evidence.

"His ultra defensive play **implied** that he was very nervous" - (correct).

"From his timid performance, I **inferred** that he must be very nervous" - (also correct).

Prevaricate or **Procrastinate** – two words, though subtly different, both refer to methods frequently employed by politicians when parrying tricky questions from tenacious interviewers. To **prevaricate** means "to avoid giving a direct or truthful answer" whereas to **procrastinate** means "to delay an action or decision until later". These are the Collins dictionary definitions which rightly maintain the core differences between the two words. The Oxford dictionary propounds more flexible interpretations and I suspect this may have helped spread the confusion. But effective communication relies on clarity of meaning. Put simply, to **prevaricate** is to lie; to **procrastinate** is to delay. Accurate speech requires these distinctions.

Wander or **Wonder** – another two useful verbs whose meanings, though widely understood, can sometimes lead to confusion through mispronunciation. To "wander" is "to move around aimlessly" - "He was **wandering** in the woods" has a clear meaning provided "**wandering**" is pronounced correctly: i.e. "wand" as in "pond". But one often hears "**wander**" pronounced as in "under" which immediately confuses it with "**wonder**" which, of course, is also pronounced as in "under". Thus the example given, if pronounced incorrectly, would suggest that he was in the woods having a good think. Please, therefore, be sure to pronounce "**wander**" correctly.

Assure, Ensure or **Insure** – here we have three similar words with meanings that differ slightly but significantly. **Assure** means "to confirm something will happen". e.g.

"I can **assure** you he will escape if you don't always keep the door locked."

"**Ensure**" means almost the same as "**assure**" but suggests that special precautions have been taken to make sure of a particular result. e.g.

"I have bought enough food to **ensure** we shall not starve while the shops are closed."

"**Insure**" suggests that a protective measure has been put in place to guard against any unfortunate future event. This will often involve taking out a formal insurance policy. Or it may entail making provision for any potentially unwanted occurrence. e.g.

"It is prudent to **insure** a boiler separately even though home insurance should give an owner sufficient cover."

N.B. An **insurance** policy gives cover if a specified event takes place.

An **assurance** policy gives persistent cover for extended periods, normally until death.

7

AMERICAN ANOMALIES

I said at the start that we were dealing with English as developed in Britain, mainly to distinguish it from American English which uses different spellings in various instances. For example, the "**u**" is normally dropped from words ending in "**our**" (British spelling). e.g. Neighbo**u**r; rumo**u**r; humo**u**r. All lose their "**u**" in America but the pronunciation is not affected. Another example would be words ending in "ise" (normal British spelling) but "**ize**" in American. e.g.

Fraterni**s**e; reali**s**e; speciali**s**e. Here the hard "**s**" is replaced by "**z**" in America. Sensibly, American English has simplified certain spellings. Indeed, there are instances where this can suggest the correct pronunciation when the British spelling can lead to ambiguity and resulting pitfalls. Take "**jewellery**" as spelt the British way but pronounced as two syllables (ignoring the final "e"). America spells it as one hears it - "**jewelry**". I'm afraid it is quite common to hear ignorant British people pronounce "**jewellery**" with three syllables (as written in the UK) but this is a blunder.

Americans may use different past participles where they spurn the shortened versions. e.g. Spelled/spelt; burned/burnt; dreamed/dreamt; learned;learnt. It should be noted that "learned" (but not "learnt") can be used as an adjective to mean well-educated. But then it must be pronounced as two syllables ("learn" and "ed") - another possible pitfall but probably a rare one.

"**Gotten**" is not accepted as a past participle of "**Get**" in Britain but it is the norm in America. The rather nasty word "got" is the past of "get" in England but it should be avoided whenever possible. e.g.

"He has never **gotten** a present from his mean brother" - acceptable in the US but not in the UK. The equivalent in British English "He has never **got** a present from his mean brother" is not technically wrong but must surely sound clumsy to any native speaker. With a little thought and discipline it is usually possible to jettison the verb "**get**" and use a more appropriate word. "He has never received a present from his mean brother" is an elegant and simple solution.

8

SOCIETY AND "CLASS" ISSUES

A class system still exists in British society in spite of widespread dumbing down and political talk about our new classless society. It is generally true that the lower classes and genuine upper classes (the nobility) do not pay much attention to their rank in society. They accept their fate and get on with life. It is the middle classes – and, in particular, those aspiring to the upper-middle category - who are most likely to continue promoting the class system and all the associated snobbery that goes with it.

In the 1950s and '60s, terms known as "U" (upper) and "Non-U" (non-upper) were popularised by Nancy Mitford in her book *Noblesse Oblige.* Aspirants to the upper echelons of society still observe the use, or otherwise, of many sensitive words (U or Non-U) with great care. Such close scrutiny should be seen as no more than a source of amusement; but it still remains a serious matter for the true snob.

For those bothered about the whole class issue and how it relates to educational attainment, the way a person speaks is generally considered to be one of the most important factors. Accent (1), pronunciation (2), grammatical structure (3) and choice of words (4) all contribute to the overall impression given.

1. We are not concerned here with accents (or dialects) other than to emphasise the importance of using distinct diction. Unintelligible words, however spoken, are no use to anyone.

2. **Pronunciation** is generally a matter of personal choice and seldom clearly right or wrong. However, in some cases of particularly slovenly speech, a lazily articulated word can have a dramatic effect on its meaning. e.g.

A couple of local lads are sitting in a pub garden. A dark cloud is drifting overhead and a waitress appears with a jug of beer. Bill says to John: "I think we're going to get some more ale". John replies: "Let's get inside quickly" and off he goes at once, leaving a bemused Bill beckoning the waitress. He had been watching her whereas John had been looking at the sky. Bill and John would both have been what are sometimes known as "H" Droppers and would seldom if ever actually pronounce an "H". Hence

John instinctively thought Bill was talking about an impending hailstorm. This is obviously an extreme example of an unlikely misunderstanding but I hope it serves its purpose.

Where to apportion stress on words with multiple syllables can sometimes cause confusion.

Longer adjectives normally require stress on the first syllable. e.g.

"**Mandatory**" should be pronounced as three syllables with the stress on "Man" and the "r" disregarded. Do not stress the "dat"!

"**Lamentable**" is four syllables with the stress on "Lam" and not on "men".

However, such distinctions are unlikely to be crucial and there are too many examples to make further consideration feasible in this short book.

3. **Grammatical Structure** has been the overriding topic and main reason for writing this book. I have explained many examples of solecisms but these are brought to your attention, not as comments on class strata, rather as examples of unacceptable ignorance.

4. **Choice of Words** does sometimes reveal a person's class and active snobs will list several words as taboo. However, most

of these words have legitimate uses provided they are applied in the right context. e.g.

"**Toilet**" comes from the French word "toilette". Though now considered archaic, it retains its original meaning - "activities and accoutrements associated with getting dressed" - and should still be used in this context. It is not needed for its common use meaning "**lavatory**" or "**loo**", both exemplary alternatives, and so in this sense "**toilet**" should be discarded once and for all. But this is not going to happen, of course. Nowadays "toilets" are posted on signs throughout Europe, if not the world. However, individuals should still refrain from saying "toilets" when they mean "lavatories".

"**Writing Paper**" is the correct description of the formal paper used when writing letters - not "**notepaper**" which is self-evidently the wrong word and should only be used for taking notes.

"**Lunch**" (or "luncheon" – meaning a more formal affair) is a meal taken in the middle of the day. "**Dinner**" is the formal meal taken in the evening or at night. It is wrong to use "dinner" for any meal eaten during the middle of the day. "Supper" should be used in place of "dinner" to describe a light meal taken in the evening.

"**Tea**", when describing a light meal (not the drink), can also be used incorrectly. Normally short for "afternoon tea", this is a typically English event (especially relished between innings in a village cricket match) comprising such delights as scones, cucumber sandwiches (finely cut brown bread, please – with crusts removed) and a selection of cakes to go with a cup of tea (or several cups). Morning tea - sometimes known as "elevenses" (signifying the time of day) - is likely to be a lesser event with a cup of tea and perhaps a biscuit or two.

"**Tea**" should not be used as an alternative word for dinner or supper and yet, in many households – particularly in northern England, it is the preferred word for an early dinner.

"**Pudding**", "**Sweet**", "**Dessert**" and "**Savoury**" – still on the eating theme, these terms

might all be used to describe particular courses that constitute a formal meal. The main course precedes the "**pudding**" or "**dessert**" which will be followed by cheese and biscuits and possibly fruit and nuts. A "**savoury**" (probably a sorbet) might be introduced at any time "to clear the palate" (perhaps to prepare for the cheese and port) and coffee and chocolates should be served to complete the feast. A variety of wines should be served throughout, each one chosen to complement the course with which it is drunk. I have tried to portray something approaching a typical British banquet.

Two more important points should be noted:

1. "**Sweet**", mentioned as part of the heading to this paragraph, is often used in place of "**pudding**" or "**dessert**". This is a mistake (and non-U!) because a **sweet** is a piece of confectionery likely to contain sugar (providing the sweet taste). Used as an adjective, it would be acceptable to proffer a sweet course – but not a **sweet,** unless you mean something like a peppermint to go with the coffee.
2. I have described this as a "British" banquet because, though likely to follow a similar format in the old British colonies, there is a notable difference wherever French influence is encountered. The French like to eat their cheese before their "**dessert**" and, as the world's leading gourmet nation, this should be taken into consideration. I believe the British developed their preference for cheese at the end because it went better with the port wine, their favoured drink to complete a serious meal.

"**Table Napkin**" (or more often simply "napkin") is what too many people call a "serviette". "**Serviette**" is a French word meaning "towel" and therefore, as well as being "non-U", does not impart an accurate meaning of "napkin". Some might say (particularly those influenced by America) that "napkin" is another word for sanitary towel but that definition is not normally used in the UK. If avoidance of ambiguity is essential, then use the correct, full term "**Table Napkin**". Others might say that "serviette" means a "paper napkin" which may often be the case; but, then again, why not use the full term "paper napkin"? Use of the word "serviette" should always be avoided (unless speaking French!).

"**Lounge**", "**Drawing Room**", "**Sitting Room**" and "**Living Room**" are all possible terms for reception rooms in a private house. The ironic thing is, though, that probably the most commonly used word of the four, "**lounge**" is the only one that should not be used for any room in a private dwelling. The correct definition of "**lounge**" is "a communal room in a hotel, ship or airport". The "**drawing room**", originally the prime room in which to withdraw, suggests an expansive house or even a mansion. The average humble cottage would not presume to boast a "**drawing room**" and would more happily settle for a "**sitting room**". Houses with a variety of reception rooms may have both, as well as a dining room and possibly a study, library, television room, etc. An all-purpose room may be called a "**living room**" but such a room would probably only be found in a small house where, as suggested, most of the living would take place.

"**Sofa**", "**Settee**" and "**Couch**" - three words with similar meanings but different uses. For an upholstered seat for at least two people, "**sofa**" is the right word . "**Settee**" means much the same though it may only be wide enough for two persons. However, the word "settee" is considered "non-U" even though it has genuine English origins. So a **sofa** specifically designed for two should rather just be called a small **sofa.** A "**couch**" differs from a **sofa** in that it does not have side or back supports and is more likely to be found in a doctor's consulting room than a private house. Therefore, a "**couch**" is not the same as a "**sofa**" and this distinction should always be observed.

9

EVOLVED MEANINGS

Most of the information given so far has promoted my desire – and I hope yours - for better spoken English. Instead of continuing this theme, in this chapter, simply out of general interest, I am going to deal with some words whose meanings have changed or increased quite dramatically in recent times.

"**Gay**" is one of the most obvious examples of a word whose original meaning has nearly disappeared. It has become the preferred term to describe a homosexual man or lesbian woman. In this modern sense it can be a noun or an adjective, whereas it used only to be an adjective meaning carefree and merry or bright and cheerful. e.g.

"*The Great Gatsby* portrayed a wonderful vision of **gay** society as found on Long Island in the 1920s." Say this to young people nowadays and they would probably assume that homosexuality was rife throughout Long Island. Sadly, it has become almost impossible to use "gay" in its traditional sense.

"**Queer**" has effectively been superseded by "gay". When society decided it needed a more succinct word to describe homosexuality, "queer" (meaning not normal or strange) became the logical choice. Like "gay" it can be used as a noun in this sense and it was not originally frowned upon as an offensive term. Unfortunately, this is no longer the case and to call someone a "queer" is extremely derogatory. However, I'm told that within homosexual society it is acceptable to call one another "queer". Queer indeed, one might say!

"**Wicked**" is an adjective normally used to describe either a human action of evil or depravity or, in its more playful mode, merely mischievous or roguish antics. e.g.

"She was back to her "wicked" ways, insisting on a skinny dip whenever there was a full moon."

However, in addition to these two normal definitions, another almost antithetical meaning has recently become increasingly popular. Anything thought to be really good is simply said to be "wicked", whether or not it refers to a human action. e.g.

"He gave her yet another glass of champagne. "Wicked" was her immediate riposte."

"**Legend**" and its adjective "**legendary**" originally referred to apocryphal tales originating centuries ago and handed down by word of mouth. Based on fact or fiction, the popularity of these stories over such a long span of time has given them a high degree of esteem. But this commendable association has increasingly been applied to people who are still alive and have somehow achieved fame. The very fact that their existence is undoubted technically denies their legendary status. King Arthur and Robin Hood are **legends**, not Elvis Presley, Roger Federer or Tiger Woods. However, I suspect this assertion will increasingly be ignored. Nowadays, I hear the younger generation even giving legendary status to their friends who have achieved no widespread fame at all.

"**Crush**" used as a verb essentially means to squeeze something with considerable force so as to change its shape or condition. e.g.

"The new machine could **crush** any scrapped vehicle within seconds." This remains the predominant meaning but it could be used in the sense of utterly defeating or destroying a person or enemy. However, "**crush**" seems to have taken on a new meaning whereby it can be used to express a winning result or successful outcome. e.g.

"Customers were literally begging to subscribe; the new advertisement had really **crushed** it." Or "You really **crushed** that drive; I've never seen you hit a golf ball that far." I suspect the use of "**crush**" in this manner has been developed by optimistic young Americans.

"**Streak**", used as a noun or verb, still suggests a line or flash showing a contrast to the predominant colour. Or it may refer to a short period of time. It is only since the 1970s that it has become synonymous with running naked through a public place. Indeed **streaking** at sports events became a bit of a fad in the '70s, '80s and '90s. However, initial amusement often turned into annoyance and perpetrators, especially less attractive ones, were generally seen as a nuisance. With this attitude and tighter security, a successful **streak** is rarely seen nowadays.

10

PRONUNCIATION AND ARTICULATION

The main purpose of this short book has been to encourage better spoken English. Typical grammatical errors have been addressed along with various words which are often misused. However, little has been said about accents or dialects because this is a complex aspect of our language beyond the scope of this treatise. Pronunciation and grammar are not necessarily correlated, though it might be assumed that a pedantic grammarian would also be a meticulous enunciator. However, although I said earlier: "pronunciation is seldom clearly right or wrong" (it being more a matter of personal choice), there are some words to which this maxim definitely does not apply. Prime examples are "hurricane" - last syllable should not be stressed (as in per<u>son</u> – **not** as in <u>cane</u>); "tortoise" and "porpoise"- last syllable pronounced as in pur<u>pose</u> – **not** as in <u>toys</u>.

There are many ways of pronouncing the written word, especially those of more than one syllable. The placing of the stress on multi-syllabic words can be important. Some variations may be equally acceptable: others may not. It is normally correct to stress the first syllable in most adjectives (cf. ch. 8); but no universal rules can be applied, either for adjectives or any other words – and certainly not for place names. Where there is ambiguity, it is often more a case of learning by association with one's peer group and then copying its most highly-regarded members. I apologise for what might be deemed vapid advice: but correct pronunciation is a subjective art form. It derives from the experience gained by individuals as they listen and learn to speak in such a manner as gives them most satisfaction.

Lots of place names have alternative pronunciations many of which have given rise to all sorts of heated arguments. Locals may insist their way is right even though it bears little resemblance to the spelling. Whole syllables can be left out as with Hunstanton in Norfolk, which is often (but not invariably) pronounced "Hunstan" by the locals. Leominster in Herefordshire should always be pronounced "Lemster". Shrewsbury, the county town of Shropshire, is pronounced as in "throw" and certainly not as in "shrew" (the little mouselike animal), as might be presumed by the ignorant. Mildenhall in Suffolk is pronounced as it is written but Mildenhall in Wiltshire is doggedly pronounced "Minal" by the locals. Gillingham in Kent has a soft "G" (as in the name "Gill") whereas Gillingham in Dorset has a hard "G" (as in the "gills" of a fish). Many more examples could be cited (most of which I wouldn't know about!) but I have tried to point out the better known and more interesting ones. Readers will assuredly have conflicting views but place names are invariably a lively subject for discussion "down the pub".

My final reference to pronunciation would confirm the fact that letters or even syllables should sometimes be omitted. I cannot think of any cases where they need to be added. But there is one common instance where an "r" seems to appear from nowhere and thus produces the horrible expression "I saw **r**it 'appen down the pub (sic)" or "he saw **r**it ...". This use of an "r" after "saw" is a strange case of non-existent alliteration which must be avoided.

Articulation – the way in which a word is delivered – differs slightly from pronunciation but has an equally important bearing on speech quality. Pronunciation is the actual sound which is heard: articulation is the quality of that sound. The purpose of speech is to convey one's thoughts to an audience. Well-constructed sentences comprising a wide and interesting vocabulary are required to achieve this aim most effectively. Indeed, the whole point of this book has been to highlight this hypothesis. But even the most erudite speaker has to articulate well to be entirely successful. As I said earlier (cf ch.8), no matter how brilliant the content, unintelligible words, however spoken, do not get the job done. Distinct diction and good voice projection are also necessary. Overcoming a stutter or stammer may need specialist therapy but good articulation simply needs practice. Slow it down and open your mouth would be my two main directives. Work on both these details should overcome any propensity to mumble and also help produce a pleasing, r**ou**nded "**ow**" s**ou**nd ("**ow**" as in "r**ou**nd" or "s**ou**nd"). Older readers may remember h**ow** Ted Heath used to struggle pron**ou**ncing this s**ou**nd, particularly when talking ab**ou**t his treasured yacht *Morning Cl**ou**d*.

It's surprising how often this "**ow**" sound crops up, so please let's articulate it correctly.

CONCLUSION

This has been a random discourse on common mistakes increasingly encountered in today's spoken English. Our wonderful language should not have to suffer this abuse. I hope that by raising awareness of some of these basic errors, correctly articulated English can be better appreciated. I also hope that sympathetic readers will spread the word and be kind enough to leave a favourable review on Amazon.

Finally, I have one last gripe (you would surely expect this!). In far too many cases "**So**" seems to have become the instinctive initial response to nearly every statement and question. It is almost universally used as an introductory gambit. This is wrong and I'm afraid I find the habit infuriating. Unless it is used as a corollary to a specific question – e.g. "Why did he climb the wall? **So** he could see what was on the other side" - it is **NOT** correct to start a sentence with "**So**"!

BIBLIOGRAPHY

Chambers Paperback Thesaurus (1991)

Collins Paperback Dictionary (4th edition, 1999)

Eats, Shoots & Leaves, by Lynne Truss (Fourth Estate, 2009)

Oxford Dictionary of English (OUP 3rd edition, 2010)

Paperback Oxford English Dictionary (OUP 7th edition, 2012)

Simply English, by Simon Heffer (Windmill Books, 2015)

Strictly English, by Simon Heffer (Windmill Books, 2011)

APPENDIX

An audible version of this book will soon be available at **audi-ble.co.uk**. You will be able to listen to me relating essentially the same script but with many pertinent embellishments. After all, I am trying to improve the standard of **spoken** English so an oral monologue should be a rewarding addition.

Printed in Great Britain
by Amazon